HOW TO BUILD SELF-KNOWLEDGE:
Discovering who you are

chad prevost

Copyright © 2020 The Big Self School

The Big Self School is a personal growth learning community, whose central mission is to help you deepen your self-knowledge so that you can improve your life. We create digital courses, online community, books, and media designed to activate self-awareness, deeper connections, bold action, and healthy habits so you can play big without burning out.

www.bigselfschool.com

Printed in the United States of America
Text layout and design: Averil Eagle Brannen
Library-of-Congress Control Number is available upon request.
ISBN: 978-1-945064-22-7
eISBN: 978-1-945064-23-4

OTHER BOOKS FROM THE BIG SELF SCHOOL:

- **DESIRE:** How Do You Want To Feel?

- **WHAT DO YOU EXPECT?** Discovering Methods For Deep Calm

- **WHO DO YOU THINK YOU ARE?** 365 meditations + the books they came from

HOW TO BUILD SELF-KNOWLEDGE:
Discovering who you are

FOREWORD

IF YOU'VE COME THIS FAR, DON'T STOP NOW.

This small book, like all the books in this series, distills a broad and complex topic into a fair and practical application. The work you put in from the starting gate of this moment will yield results for years. You're right on the cusp of a whole universe of self-knowledge. You may think you know the subject well, but you almost certainly don't. The subject is even more complicated and fascinating. The subject is you.

If you've come this far, don't stop now. Visualize sunlight splintering through a lifting fog, clouds clearing. Visualize boarding a train. You drop off your baggage with the handler.

Enter with openness, with no expectations. Enter only with the intention not to stop until you've arrived at your destination. Only you know when that is.

The pursuit of self-knowledge has the potential to help you confront and resolve personal issues no matter how painful or deep they may be. These are obstacles obscuring your path to understanding what philosophers and psychologists call the true self (which we define ahead). While you can't change the things you wished never happened to you, you can change your perception. You can grow. You can heal.

Self-knowledge provides you with the tools and the ability to change your perception, to rid yourself of baggage carried within your mind for so long, bringing peace and integration of all parts of yourself into your life. In going to the source, toward root causes, you can bring about a permanent change in your perception and understanding of your pain, its cause and its resolution.

The train is leaving the station. Time to hop on board.

ONE

How little we know

If you've only just begun the self-knowledge journey you may be surprised to learn that it is incredibly difficult to know yourself. Lao Tzu, the ancient Chinese philosopher, who lived in the 6th century BCE, wrote, "He who knows others is wise; he who knows himself is enlightened." Similarly, Carl Jung said, "Who looks outside, dreams; who looks inside, awakes." The sum total of philosophic inquiry is said to have been summarized by Socrates who said, "Know thyself." Plato similarly phrased it, "The unexamined life is not worth living."

Why? Because the self is a wilderness.

Contemporary psychology has fundamentally questioned the notion that we can know ourselves objectively and with finality. It has argued that the self is not so much a "thing" as it is a process of continual adaptation to changing circumstances. And the fact that we so often see ourselves as more competent, moral, and stable than we actually are serves our ability to adapt. Some even point out that a fair amount of self-delusion and self-ignorance is actually helpful to this extent.

While psychology over the past two centuries has contributed the most in the realm of self-knowledge, we would do well to begin with philosophy's contribution. In philosophy, self-knowledge generally refers to knowledge of one's own sensations, thoughts, beliefs, and other mental states. At least since Descartes, most philosophers have believed that our knowledge of our own mental states differs markedly from our knowledge of the external world, which includes our knowledge of others' thoughts.

But there is little agreement about what distinguishes self-knowledge from knowledge of anything else. Partly for this reason, philosophers endorse competing accounts of how we acquire self-knowledge. The most famous argument on self-knowledge is the certainty of a particular instance of belief. This is Descartes' "cogito argument," which demonstrates that so long as you carefully attend to your own thoughts, nothing can prove that you are not thinking and, therefore, you exist.

Perhaps the most widely accepted view along these lines is that self-knowledge, even if not absolutely certain, is especially secure, in the following sense: self-knowledge is immune from some types of error to which other kinds of empirical knowledge — most obviously, perceptual knowledge — are vulnerable. That is where inferential ways of knowing become the primary way for us to suggest that we can know the self. That is where the term "looking within" uses a spatial comparison to express a divide between the "inner" world of thought and the "external" world.

Self-knowledge is a skill, not a trait, talent, or divine insight.

Self-ignorance

Your self does not lie before you like an open book. You can't just open up the hatch in the back of your skull and root around until you locate your "self." Think of all the self-portraits of artists over the centuries. A "portrait of the artist as a young self" has become almost a rite of passage for writers and artists. The attempt to look at yourself is fraught with much more difficulty than looking outward. It can be frightening to look within. We may not like what we see.

We are often blind to ourselves and the effect we have on others because we literally do not see our own facial expressions, gestures, and body language. You may be barely aware that your blinking eyes indicate stress. You may not hear how your tone communicates much more than the actual words you say. The same is true of all kinds of body language. The slump in your posture betrays something that weighs on you.

Princeton University psychologist, Emily Pronin, calls the mistaken belief in privileged access the "introspection illusion." The way we view ourselves is distorted, and we don't realize it. Our self-image has little to do with our actions. We may see ourselves in a way that stands in complete contradiction to the way we live. We may say we love the outdoors but never do anything outside. We may say we value time with family, but give all our enthusiasm to our job or personal pursuits. We may believe we're a talented artist even though we don't produce any art.

There are many ways we construct false narratives about ourselves. We tell ourselves the potential is within us, but we just never have the time. We tell ourselves forces outside us compel us to behave in ways that aren't truly "who we are." These truth distortions aren't necessarily wrong. The question is how we lie to ourselves or distort our self's reality, but why?

Let us begin with the simple premise that the pursuit of self-knowledge is practical. You will be happier and more effective in your life if you know yourself.

Strangely enough, in order to succeed at things that are going to be fraught with challenge and possibly hardship, you might need to possess a little delusion. Elizabeth Dunn and Timothy Wilson report that mild self-illusions can be beneficial.

It's not always to your benefit to know just how stacked the odds are against success in your field. Is it always good to know how many more talented baseball players have tried to make it to the major leagues if that is something you aspire to? If you want to succeed in the music industry do you really need to know how much more talented thousands of people are than you before you start putting in your daily practice? Sometimes, as with running up a long hill, it's better to see just enough in front of you to take the next step and keep on moving.

Extreme self-illusions, on the other hand, can undermine well-being. If you're small and slow, it's probably not the healthiest to dream you can play for the NBA. If you value great wealth and having lots of things, but you just like watering your ferns, petting your cat, and making grilled cheese sandwiches, you may not possess the drive it takes — or find pleasure in what you're doing that could bring you greater wellbeing.

Overall, self-knowledge is better for you than self-ignorance. It's probably impossible to go through life without any self-beliefs, so this is a fair enough starting point. When it comes to knowing yourself ignorance is not bliss.

Without splitting philosophic hairs, let's start with this premise: You are no more or less than the sum of your thoughts, actions, attitudes, emotions, abilities, values, and physical characteristics.

With this in mind, you can begin to paint a portrait of yourself that lines up with your inner and outer reality. What you seek is a self that integrates these pieces of you.

Albert Einstein once said, "No problem can be solved from the same level of consciousness that created it," and that is exactly why we access our depths through other forms of consciousness. When you continue to ask the same questions and make the same choices, you get the same results. To move in a different direction requires insight into where you have been and where you are, clarity on what no longer serves, and direction on how to move into where you would like to be.

Self-knowledge will make you a better person

Tasha Eurich has made a career demonstrating the strong links with scientific evidence that people are happier when they know themselves and how others see them. They are better decision-makers. They have better personal and professional relationships. They raise more mature children. They become smarter, more adept students who choose better careers. They also tend to be more creative, confident, and overall better communicators. And because knowing yourself does require a sophisticated level of learning and understanding, you also learn about the fundamentals of morality.

Daniel Goleman, one of the pioneers of Emotional Intelligence Theory, says that recent advancements in positive psychology have made self-awareness more accessible than ever. Goleman suggests that self-awareness is one of the four main pillars of emotional intelligence, and is imperative for success in any field. Most people think emotional intelligence is about managing other people's emotions. Identifying and managing your own emotions is paramount first and foremost.

It's not so much that you live up to a perceived ideal of "authenticity." Knowing yourself means recognizing when disparities occur between who you aspire to be and how you live out your life. People who know themselves well also tend to be less aggressive and less likely to lie, cheat, and steal. When your values line up in integration with your work situations you tend to be a better performer, one more likely to get a promotion. People who know themselves well are more effective leaders with more enthusiastic employees. Research even shows that self-awareness is the single greatest predictor of leadership success.

Our wellbeing grows as our conscious goals and unconscious motives become more integrated. But if you can't fully trust yourself to tell you who you are, then who can you trust?

The answer is: Others.

But what do others know anyway? Aren't "others" the very ones we like to criticize and judge?

"Is it me, or is your response really about you?"

Life is complicated. People are complicated. On the one hand, with people's responses, it's really not about you. But almost as soon as that idea begins to absorb, we have to para-doxically remind ourselves that, truth be told, it is sometimes about us. Sometimes we do create the conditions for the reality we experience. The wisdom is in learning to know the difference.

As an editor for a magazine, and later of an independent publishing house, I frequently found myself on panels discuss-ing how and why a work is accepted for publishing. As a writer myself, I would frequently find myself as surprised by the content that was taken as by what wasn't. One thing I did know was that a person's work isn't observed in a vacuum. There is always context.

Your work may be read in the morning or afternoon, which has an impact on the freshness of the editor's reading. It could have been the first in the stack or 41st. It could have been among 41 other entries or 4,001. It could have been on a topic that was thematically in line with the values of the editor — or just the opposite. One editor may like tightly-constructed sentences, and another may like a discursive, associative style. Does an editor believe this work will contribute to the marketplace (be sellable), or is it art for art's sake? There are nearly limitless reasons for acceptance or rejection that may have little to nothing to do with the quality of the work.

Similarly with teaching. While good teaching is about patience and clarity, the art and science of challenging and encouraging students, you may be meeting a student at a time when they are eager and ready to learn, or at a time when the field is fallow. I've also had back-to-back classes in which I would teach the exact same thing with the exact same level of enthusiasm, and with the exact same punchlines, and the reactions of the class were entirely different. The class that laughs at your every joke and eagerly asks questions and raises their hands to contribute to the discussion energizes you. They make you feel like you can do no wrong and what a joy teaching is. The reserved, non-responsive ones make you aware of the sweat that's breaking out on your forehead as you try to persevere.

Good work is good work, but what we can't control are the responses from others to the work. The same is true of the processes we put in ourselves. That is why a Stoic-influenced perspective suggests that maintaining your own values and priorities is all the reward you need. In those cases, adjust your expectations. Realize it is not about you. It's about them.

Until that is, you run into the occasions where it really is about you.

One of the earliest leading indicators that an issue lies within ourselves is when we repeatedly experience the same type of conflict with others. Most people have a vague sense of their behaviors but remain more or less exactly the same year after year. In general, this is because it takes real courage to look at long unexamined (or perhaps never examined) shadow sides of ourselves. We don't like these parts of ourselves, much less admitting to them. It doesn't feel good, and it's hard to go to the source and bring up unconscious things over and over again to reflect on them and analyze them in order to create any real change.

The freedom you gain from breaking a pattern often brings great relief, like a burden has been lifted. We have seen those who put in the work find enormous releases of stress. When the breakthrough happens, and when you're able to step back and recognize it, few things bring on as much calm. Calm is one of the building blocks for the development of self-knowledge.

Of course there are the rare occasions where even when you do have a repeated issue with others it is because you are taking a personal stand for a principled reason. If you are sure you are right, don't let the world get in the way. Don't let your friends or family swerve you for a moment from your purpose.

Becoming self-aware is the basic foundation for creating the life you want. Your happiness depends on it.

But improving your self-knowledge won't happen in a day. Sometimes it takes years of reflection, introspection, and difficult conversations with people you affect directly or indirectly. As you grow in self-awareness, you will find you get more comfortable being your true self, transparent, and even vulnerable. You will have more acceptance of yourself, and more acceptance and others. You will also have more insight into discerning when others are telling you something you need to hear, and when it is really about them.

What meditation does and doesn't do

The past decade saw a proliferation of neuroscience studies with widespread optimism about what we could "prove" is going on in the brain during activities in which the brain is at work but the body is otherwise seen to be "calm" or in stasis. The problem is that there is a fundamental divide between brain study and what the "mind" is actually doing when it is in the process of meditating. Making it even further complicated, there are many ways to meditate. (We offer an approach in the third section of this book.)

Most neuroscience research has so far focused on mindfulness, and that has generally shown positive results. Mindfulness in meditation beginners has been linked to increases in the anterior cingulate cortex activation (easy for me to say!), which is associated with attention control, and deactivation in the amygdala (aka: reptilian), associated with threat detection.

In 2013, Erika Carlson reviewed the literature on whether and how mindfulness meditation improves one's self-knowledge. Her research suggests that the construct of mindfulness, defined as paying attention to one's current experience in a non-evaluative way, may serve as a path to self-knowledge.

Specifically, mindfulness appears to directly address two major barriers to self-knowledge: informational barriers (the quantity and quality of information people have about themselves), and motivational barriers (ego-protective motives that affect how people process information about themselves). Mindfulness can clarify your thinking and dissolve your ego's protective shell. The practice of mindfulness teaches you how to allow your thoughts to simply drift by and to identify with them as little as possible. Thoughts are, after all, transitory and not absolute truth.

Before we offer the benefits of meditation, it should also be said that meditation isn't always a pleasant experience. Recently, researchers from University College London in the UK set out to discover the answer more scientifically from conducting a survey of over 1,200 participants. The team found that over 25% who regularly meditate had a negative experience including "feelings of fear and distorted emotions."

How do you define an unpleasant experience? The challenge of emotional confrontation doesn't feel good, especially at first. We suggest leaning into the challenge, rather than deciding it must be a reason to stop. Sometimes you do need a guide. Sometimes you do need a therapist. You need to be comfortable with dealing with emotions in the first place. It helps to have a framework. The study showed that those with a religious belief were less likely to have a negative experience. Women also reported fewer negative experiences.

More research is needed. With that said, much of the mindfulness research that has been conducted points to many positive benefits, all of which should be considered.

Through our podcast network at Big Self, we have discussed the benefits and practices of meditation with healthcare practitioners such as Matt McClanahan, Kristi Angevine, Patricia McClelland, as well as other theorists, scholars, and coaches. They report a variety of meditation practices that build your ability to redirect and maintain attention. The improved focus you can gain through regular meditation may increase memory and mental clarity. Metta, or "lovingkindness" meditation, is a practice of developing positive feelings, first toward yourself and then toward others. Positivity toward others develops a natural extension toward empathy and compassion.

Many styles of meditation can help reduce stress, anxiety, and anxiety-related mental health issues. Some forms of meditation improve depression and help people reframe their outlook. Self-inquiry and related styles of meditation can help you "know yourself." Self-observation and depersonalizing our thoughts and emotions from who we are as a self is important. Many inputs shape the self. Sometimes meditation is nothing more than detaching and observing.

Overall, meditation develops mental discipline and willpower and can help you avoid triggers for unwanted impulses. This can help you recover from addiction, lose weight, and redirect unwanted habits. Meditation techniques can help you relax and control thoughts that interfere with sleep. This can shorten the time it takes to fall asleep and increase sleep quality. Meditation has also been shown to diminish the perception of pain in the brain. This may help treat chronic pain when used as a supplement to medical care or physical therapy.

The true self is the moral self

"To thine own self be true," says Shakespeare's Polonius. Given that Polonius was a windbag full of empty platitudes, the statement has a more negative association than the average reader who sees the quote floating past on an inspirational Tweet might perceive. But what is the true self to which we should be true? Does it exist? And how do you know if and when you're being "true" to your "self" as opposed to being untrue, fake, or inauthentic?

Walt Whitman said he "contains multitudes," and the same could be said for the self — for any self. The self is a body and mind. We are full of desires, wants and needs, as well as the thoughts that are considered conscious and those that are considered unconscious, or automatic, or reflexive.

Neuroscientists, psychologists, and philosophers continue to study the concept of the self (and they probably always will). While it is virtuous to know our terms and inquire into the nature of reality, a deep-dive into the topic of the "self" can also become more about sophistry and what we can do with language, than about getting closer to a workable definition. It is equivalent to inquiring into the precise length of a nondescript piece of string, or asking for the best way to get into "the pursuit of happiness" or defining abstractions like "freedom" or "sweetness."

Should we quibble with the fact that from a very early age we recognize ourselves in the mirror? Chimpanzees, dolphins, and elephants have all passed the mirror test too, but is that the kind of self-awareness we're talking about? The levels of self-awareness in a nutshell: that's a mirror (Level 1), there's a person in it (Level 2), that person is me (Level 3), that person is going to be me forever (Level 4), and everyone else sees me (Level 5). Level 5 takes a little while to develop, usually around the age of four or five. Level 3 self-awareness is usually arrived at by 18 months. This may also be why 18- months-old is when most children begin to develop language skills. Language requires "a theory of the self as distinct from other people, and a theory of the self from the point of view of one's conversational partners," cognitive scientist Elizabeth Bates wrote in 1990.

Now that we've established our aim for a practical definition, and separated the idea of self from true self, we're ready to take the big step: Establishing what we mean by the true or authentic self.

Most people believe they have an essential core, a true self. Who they are fundamentally is demonstrated primarily in their moral values, and that seems to remain relatively stable over time and experience. Preferences, tastes, opinions may change, but the true self remains the same. Of course that most people believe in the true self doesn't make it any more or less "true." Books like *The Self Illusion* and *The Ego Trick* set out to make a case that there is no centralized self operating either in the brain or as that special "inner voice." And in recent years, it has become popular among researchers and writers to dismiss the idea that we have a "self." Although, somewhat patronizingly, it is suggested that belief in a true self may nevertheless be helpful.

Nina Strohminger, George Newman, and Joshua Knobe published an influential 2017 study, "The True Self: A Psychological Concept Distinct from the Self." They found that people typically think humans harbor a true self that is morally good. The core of the work shows our tendency to think that, in the privacy of their innermost selves, people pull for what is virtuous. People tend to consider that the true self has been altered if a person's moral sense is changed. Strohminger and her colleagues, however, conclude that we can never "prove" the existence of this self due to the "radical subjectivity and unverifiability" of the self as a scientific subject. Fair enough.

Recent literature is rife with examples of how we equate virtuous actions and beliefs with the "true" self. It crosses cultures.

There is no precise way to understand how the concept of the moral self develops. It would seem to be a way we guide ourselves toward joy, calm and resiliency, and feelings of well-being. It doesn't always translate as an inner voice, although it functions this way for many.

There are, however, other forms of inner voices that are destructive. Broadly speaking, we can call them the inner critic. We pick them up from authority figures and people who make an impression on us in our early life for one reason or another. It could be through repetition or through standout emotional experiences. Through whatever consciousness we acquired them, they are in us now. There are ways to challenge the inner critic.

Which wolf do you feed?

For many, the inner voice is generally loving and encouraging, maybe not enthusiastic, but in your corner, calmly evaluating. In fact, a good internal dialog should function much like a reasonable judge. Or like Lester Bangs tells his young protege William Miller in *Almost Famous*, "I know you think those guys are your friends. You wanna be a true friend to them? Be honest, and unmerciful." In other words, sometimes you need a good truth-telling even if it's not what you want to hear.

With that said, there is a reason we universally struggle. Struggle implies conflict. And conflict with the self, with what we call inner conflict. An old Cherokee told his grandson, "My son, there is a battle between two wolves inside us all. One is evil. It is anger, jealousy, greed, resentment, inferiority, lies, and ego. The other is good. It is joy, peace, love, hope, humility, kindness, empathy, and truth."

"Grandfather, which wolf wins?" the boy asked.

"The one you feed," the old man answered.

In order to feed the wolf that brings about integration with the true self, we must learn to listen to ourselves, to isolate the helpful inner voices from the unhelpful. Like many processes, this is easier said than done.

Not everyone is aware of their internal voice, while others are highly sensitive not only to any one voice but many. Artists and writers have compiled a great deal of material on how to listen to the gentle, compassionate, intuitive voice when needing to create, but tuning into the coldly rational and analytic one when it comes to evaluating the creation itself. Some suggest imagining the critical voices that crop up each time you approach your work and putting the voices in a jar, screwing the lid on the jar, and throwing it away. Perhaps some can find efficacy temporarily from such techniques.

Overall, however, you have to be your own friend. You have to be on your own side. You have to show love and compassion for yourself as if you were an excellent friend to yourself. In *Bird by Bird* Ann Lamott writes, "You get your confidence and intuition back by trusting yourself, by being militantly on your own side."

For some of us, we wake up one day and realize we more or less have a good wolf inside us, and it is not hard to go on feeding it, exercising it, rubbing its belly and letting it sit beside us on the couch as we binge-watch a Netflix series munching jalapeno Cheetos. For many others, we realize the bad wolf is getting scary big. It's dominant and wants all the food. The experiences that have led you to this moment have brought voices that are keeping you from integrating your true self. Still for others there may not be clarity or awareness of a wolf one way or another.

Whatever the case of the inherent self-love/hate of your inner voice, there is more good news. You are more adaptive than you probably realize. Listening to the voice that brings you strength and wholeness can be developed and learned. You can learn to tame the bad wolf and nourish and grow the good one. Some of these techniques we discuss in the final section on active reflective writing.

In order to assess the sound of our inner voices, and tune in to them, we have to turn on our radio receiver. In a calm state of mind, and in a quiet moment, ask yourself what your inner voice says when:

I feel lazy?
I have a breakthrough and achieve something?
I am stuck?
Someone else succeeds at something I want to be good at?
I think of what I want sexually?
I think about taking a risk and pursuing a dream?

What does the inner voice sound like? Is it kind and fair? Easy-going? Harsh? Is it impossible to please?

If you can really listen to the sound of your inner voice, who would you ascribe it to? Who does it sound most like?

We will always have tensions and struggles with the voices inside us. There is no ultimate utopia where we have arrived and worked our way beyond the struggle. That is when life is over. Train your mind to stop reacting and start reflecting. Train your mind to stop hiding and being cowed into submission. Train your mind to start naming and claiming the person you want to be. As V.S. Naipaul wrote, "The only lies for which we are truly punished are those we tell ourselves."

You are the director of your voices.

Frame your own story

There is another bold concept to consider. What if we quite consciously choose to create our own story? What if we choose to take matters into our own hands, and represent ourselves to the world in a way in which we dictate the terms? Would this be inauthentic? Would it be just another mask? Could it actually shape our reality, and, therefore, "who" we are?

These are important questions to consider because our experiences in life are not only shaped by the stories we tell ourselves. The stories we tell others can be just as important for a variety of reasons.

In *The 48 Laws of Power*, Robert Greene's 25th law, "Re-create Yourself," has fascinating insights into the idea of representing "who you are." While you certainly have a personality, however fluid it may be, and you do have a true self, however hard it may be to pin down scientifically, there is also this reality check: The world wants to assign you a role in life.

More good news: You don't have to accept it.

Greene suggests seizing the "Promethean task" and taking control of the process of how others see you. Especially when it comes to working within the realm of power and politics it is wise to know when you can and can't be your true self. Shape your image and force the world to respond to you, rather than the other way around. Be aware of your audience, of what will please them, and what will bore them. This creative task is like that of an artist, and you are responsible for your own creation.

Even if you believe you have no interest in playing a public-facing role of any kind, consider again that you are already telling a story — to yourself and others — about yourself. Author Michael Lewis speaks directly to it on *The Tim Ferris Show*, episode #427:

> As I've gotten older — I would say starting in my mid-to-late 20s — I could not help but notice the effect on people of the stories they told about themselves. If you listen to people, if you just sit and listen, you'll find that there are patterns in the way they talk about themselves.
>
> There's the kind of person who is always the victim in any story that they tell. Always on the receiving end of some injustice. There's the person who's always kind of the hero of every story they tell. There's the smart person; they delivered the clever put down there.

There are lots of versions of this, and you've got to be very careful about how you tell these stories because it starts to become you. You are — in the way you craft your narrative — kind of crafting your character. And so I did at some point decide, 'I am going to adopt self-consciously as my narrative, that I'm the happiest person anybody knows.' And it is amazing how happy-inducing it is.

Remember, you are the director here. Nothing has to be set in stone. You can remain true to yourself and adapt to situations for whatever the moment may require — and the better you know yourself, the better able you can frame when you're playing a role.

Mind like water

In order to think realistically about growing beyond critical voices, one important principle should be clearly discerned here. It is a concept Carol Dweck has popularized, the growth mindset versus the fixed or rigid mindset. Similarly, as the 20th-century martial artist and actor, Bruce Lee refrained: "Have a mind like water, my friends."

Carol Dweck's studies of students, men and women, parents and teachers, distills into this fundamental principle: People with a rigid sense of self take failure badly. They see it as evidence of their limitations and fear it. Fear of failure causes failure. On the other hand, those who understand that a partic-ular talent can be developed accept setbacks as information on how to do better next time. A mind like water means taking on the shape of the vessel you're poured into, being aban-doned to adaptability.

Many other studies have shown that even if we have rigid responses in some areas of our lives, we may have adaptive and clear senses of positive self-regard in others. Be open to experience, and learn to cultivate a positive voice.

But how do we get into fixed mindsets in the first place? We all want answers, but many require definitive answers. We want things black and white so they can form their identity with what seems like clarity and be comfortable in a confined scope of knowledge and understanding. The root cause is always fear. Things that are unknowable create anxiety rooted in fear. The only way out is to create a false sense of security through a framework that appears to create order — or perhaps does create an order, however limited.

I believe _____ and I am right, and those who believe _____ are wrong.
It is a waste of time to draw, not when I need to make a living. I should never speak in front of people because I get so nervous when I speak out. I will never run because I am in such poor shape it wouldn't be worth the effort.
I am naturally good at whatever I do, there is no need to chase excellence.

We want to recognize our particular traits and preferences so we can act accordingly. We tell ourselves it's a sensible response in a chaotic and uncertain world. We have certain beliefs about ourselves or the world and we're threatened when other information may conflict with those beliefs — even if they're apparently positive self-beliefs. These narratives keep us fixed in place. Growth comes slowly or not at all.

TWO

The Enneagram's versatility for understanding yourself and others

For the exploration of the self and building self-knowledge there is no tool quite like the Enneagram. It is a great place for many to start. In nearly two decades as a licensed mental health professional, and the hundreds of different types of assessments and measurements my wife and co-founder has engaged with, Shelley finds the Enneagram the richest tool. I admit I was skeptical at first, but through research, study, and personal experience, I have found it rewarding and generative not only for how I understand myself but also others.

At the same time, before we can begin the challenging work of self-understanding, we have to clear through the baggage associated with the Enneagram itself. The Enneagram's roots are deep. They are often associated with mysticism. Its influences come from both eastern and western religions. For different reasons this scares many would-be Enneagram students. On top of that there is the growing hype. With anything that gains mainstream acceptance there are blessings and curses.

The good part about its current pop status is that it demonstrates a hunger for authoritative sources for deeper understanding culturally speaking. The bad part is that it is frequently misused. People who are eager to type themselves use it more as a schematic mold rather than an organic source, which continues to reveal as understanding grows.

Right now, you can find blog posts on everything from "what sexual positions each Enneagram type prefers" to "how to organize your home based on your type." The types of content you might come across range from sheer shallow entertainment to overly-prescriptive and often weighed down with academic or religious rhetoric. It can feel like amateur-hour for a variety of reasons.

Maybe I should step back here for a moment and illustrate how the variety and richness of the Enneagram's sources are actually a sign of its versatility and strength. The roots of its sources go back at least as far as the early monastics — often called the Desert Fathers — and some scholars suggest it dates back to ancient Greeks.

Plato discussed the idea of the nine types as the Divine Forms or Platonic Solids, qualities of existence that are essential, that cannot be broken down into constituent parts. This idea was further developed in the third century by Neoplatonic philosophers, particularly Plotinus in his central work, The Enneads. From there it may have been passed on in oral tradition through the Islamic wisdom tradition of Sufism.

No doubt it is most widely associated with Christianity, but the trace elements from mystical traditions of major religions are just some of the reasons why Enneagram enthusiasts emerge from such rich and varied philosophical and religious back-grounds. You could argue that such a wide-reaching instru-ment means it has less baggage than many other instruments. Popular psychology tests such as the Meyers-Briggs, which are stripped of any apparent philosophical background could in fact be seen as a limitation in terms of their universal applica-tion. In the end, it is a useful tool, a theory without a specified origin. Like any model it is not perfect, but it is useful toward the goal of building self-knowledge.

You could say a person's Enneagram number is like a mask — a lens through which to filter the world and a facade put on at a very early age. The goal of discerning and understanding your number is to use this knowledge to remove that mask and become more of your holistic true self. Some suggest we are already imprinted "acorns" and that we were going to move through and interpret the world in one of the nine ways (27+ when you consider the subtypes). Others suggest we develop into these numbers based upon how our flawed selves interact with and respond to the flawed world. Rich-ard Rohr provides a daily email newsletter, which explores the variegated world of Enneagram interpretation. He has suggested we ultimately inhabit all the numbers, or our truest self aspires to do so, and our specific number is simply a prime characteristic, a beginning point of sorts.

Another objective of the Enneagram, aside from maturing beyond the limits of your own personality, is to use Enneagram knowledge to improve relationships with others. Learning how another person works, and how their Enneagram type is masking who they truly are, gives you a level of compassion for humanity that you have never had before. Like any other cognitive model the Enneagram is a way of interacting and understanding others and yourself. That is why the tool is fascinating no matter what number you are learning about. It's not just a "seek and find" for your own number. Each number is a description of someone we know or have known. A richer understanding of who people are, what gets them excited, what stresses them, with the corresponding "why" behind the behavior develops empathy and compassion for others.

The guidance of this book can set you on your way, and probably help you find your number without taking a test. The interpretation and phrasing of test questions often get in the way of an accurate assessment in the first place.

However, if you do want to take a test, we suggest the WEPSS. It's the only peer-reviewed Enneagram test available. That means it's the most reliable and valid. You can learn about why and how by going to the WEPSS site. We also suggest the Enneagram Institute.

Other excellent resources from which we have drawn:

The Complete Enneagram: 27 Paths to Greater Self-Knowledge
by Beatrice Chestnut

Personality Types: Using the Enneagram for Self-Discovery
by Don Richard Riso and Russ Hudson
(also by the same authors: *The Wisdom of the Enneagram: The Complete Guide to Psychological* and *Spiritual Growth for the Nine Personality Types*)

The Enneagram: A Christian Perspective
by Richard Rohr and Andreas Ebert

The Road Back to You: An Enneagram Journey to Self-Discovery
by Ian Morgan Cron and Suzanne Stabile

The Sacred Enneagram and The Enneagram of Belonging
by Chris Heuertz

Descriptions of the nine types

The Enneagram is visually represented by a circle with nine points around the circumference. Each number is connected to two other numbers by an arrow and these arrows represent the dynamic relationship between these numbers. Each number makes a move to one number when it must care for itself (a stress move) and to another number to experience holistic healing (a security move). Recent developments in the theory show that actually the "stress" move can also be a unique movement toward spiritual growth, a direction that is required for wholeness.

Each number on the Enneagram is a unique combination of a stance and a triad. For example, a four such as myself resides in the Heart, which is located in the Feeling triad (sometimes referred to as the "shame" or "sadness" triad) and has a withdrawing stance.

Wings are the numbers on either side of your number. Your wing may shift at different points in your life. For instance, as a 4 (the Romantic or Individualist), I had more closely identified with my 5 wing (the Investigator) for years as a researcher and writer. My 3 wing (the Performer) was less developed, though it would come out at times when I did public readings, or (sometimes) when I would lead classes, or played in rock bands.

One of the things I love about the Enneagram is the way it captures the fluidness of the human personality. Not only does it account for changes in one's life context over time, but it also accounts for whether a person's number is functioning on a spectrum between healthy and unhealthy, or somewhere in between. You can be a 2 in "stress" or in "growth," for instance, and it accounts for how your number tends toward other responses whether or not you're in stress or growth.

Enneagram type quick descriptions

No type is better or worse. Each has unique motivations, strengths, and weaknesses. The types transcend cultures and are without gender bias.

TYPE 1 — THE PERFECTIONIST
Fixated on improvement, as nothing is ever quite good enough. Motivated to reform and improve the world and self and avoid fault and blame.

TYPE 2 — THE HELPER
Need to be needed, and feel they are worthy insofar as they are helpful to others. Motivated to put others' needs above their own.

TYPE 3 — THE PERFORMER
Need validation to feel worthy. Motivated to pursue success and want to be admired and avoid failure. They are frequently hard working and competitive.

TYPE 4 — THE ROMANTIC
Fixated on the need to be unique and different, often creative, sensitive, and moody. Self-consciously individualistic and avoid being ordinary.

TYPE 5 — THE INVESTIGATOR

Thinkers with a detached, withdrawn stance. Motivated to learn as much as they can and conserve their energy so as not to rely on others.

TYPE 6 — THE LOYALIST

Ambivalent about others. Committed when trust is earned. Often practical and witty, motivated by fear avoidance. Worst-case thinkers who pursue security.

TYPE 7 — THE ENTHUSIAST

Life is an adventure. Often extroverted, multi-talented, creative, and open-minded. Spontaneous, but also plan for experiences. Pain avoidant.

TYPE 8 — THE CHALLENGER

Strong-willed, decisive, practical, tough-minded and energetic. Take charge to avoid being controlled. Fear feeling weak or vulnerable.

TYPE 9 — THE PEACEMAKER

Avoid conflict at all costs, whether internal or interpersonal. Pleasant and accommodating, motivated to relate to others.

You may be getting a sense of your number already, but the Enneagram is far more than a quick summary of clever names. Next, consider the stances and the triads for further clarity before trying to nail down your type.

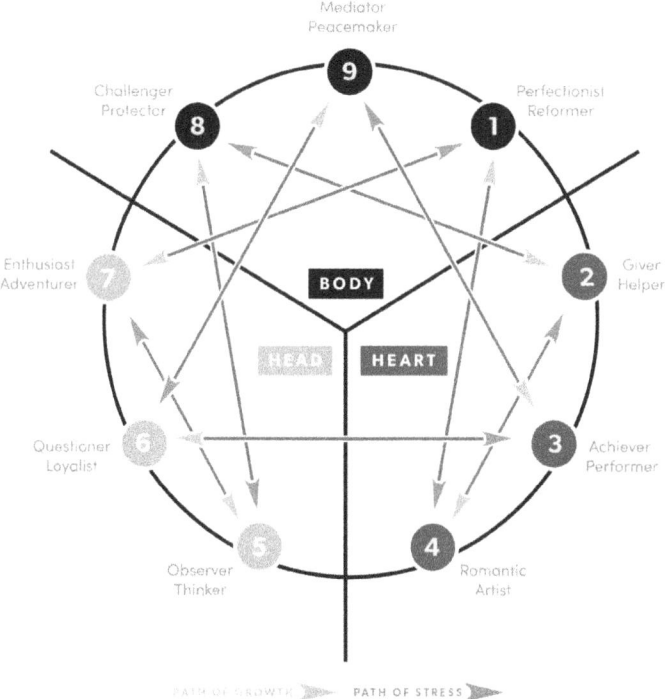

The three stances

A person's stance is how they move through the world.

People in the aggressive stance might display some or all of the following traits:

1. When they walk into a room they garner attention quickly without looking like their putting forth the effort to do so.

2. They seem to have a lot of never-ending energy.

3. They are skilled at orienting others to their own ideas, which comes off as pushy, and are excellent at reframing and reshaping situations into a positive light.

4. They prefer to say too little over too much and protect themselves with humor.

5. They are upbeat and optimistic and make people feel safe but don't intuitively connect with the feelings of others.

6. They are all about control and feel that other people move too slowly for them.

DEPENDENT STANCE

An individual in the dependent stance might display some or all of the following traits:

1. They are always thinking "What should be done next?"

2. They place their life's reference point outside of themselves and are all about other people.

3. They are concerned about your feelings and want to respond to other people in a way that is good for everyone.

4. They are good at connecting everyone and everything and sometimes chain things together that are not related at all.

5. They have trouble with their own boundaries and people with established boundaries often hurt their feelings.

WITHDRAWING STANCE

An individual in the withdrawing stance might display some or all of the following traits:

1. They are independent and non-aggressive and count on their own strength and knowledge to deal with stressful situations.

2. They are aware that there is a lot around them that needs to be done, but that their presence doesn't make a difference.

3. Their inner world is their real world because they don't connect to people easily.

4. They handle difficult situations with resentful accommodations.

5. They have lots of daydreams and inner thoughts and deal with stress by pulling back and not dealing with it.

The three triads

Just like there are three stances, there are also three triads. These triads are determined by which center (your head, heart, or gut) you filter life through first.

People in the head triad:

1. Make mental connections not easily seen by others.

2. Live by a specific plan.

3. Have no idea how much they are truly valued.

4. Keep thinking about something after others have moved on.

5. Are suspicious of others' motives.

6. Observe rather than relate.

7. Privately worry that they are wrong.

People in the head triad filter information through their thoughts first, before deciding how to react or feel about it. Fives tend to externalize the fear drive, sixes internalize, and sevens overlook it.

THE FEELING OR HEART TRIAD (TYPES 2, 3, 4)

People in the heart triad:

1. Believe that connection with others is more important than anything else.

2. Worry about how they are perceived.

3. Play out their emotions by externalizing them, internalizing them, or forget them altogether.

4. Very familiar with anxiety and how it affects them.

5. Have a hard time asking for help.

6. Need to be relationally connected.

People in the heart triad are led by their heart and tend to be the most image-conscious of the types. Twos externalize their feelings, focusing on others. Threes avoid recognizing their own or others' feelings. Fours internalize, focusing on their own feelings.

THE ANGER OR GUT TRIAD (TYPES 8, 9, 1)

People in the gut triad:

1. Feel the world with their belly and have true gut instincts.

2. Try to control both their inner world and their outer world.

3. Convert lots of emotions into anger.

4. Follow an instinctual hunch.

5. Do their part and everyone else's part.

6. Want to impact the world and dismiss you/others in the process.

People in the gut triad have a gut reaction first and tend to express themselves with directness and honesty. Eights externalize their anger. Nines repress it. Ones internalize it.

Finding your number

Each Enneagram type is a unique combination of one stance and one triad. Reference what you wrote down as your stance and combine it with your triad to find your number. The list starts with eight to keep the three triad types together.

The numbers go as follows:

Eight: Aggressive Stance: Gut Triad
Nine: Withdrawing Stance: Gut Triad
One: Dependent Stance: Gut Triad

Two: Dependent Stance: Heart Triad
Three: Aggressive Stance: Heart Triad
Four: Withdrawing Stance: Heart triad

Five: Withdrawing Stance: Head Triad
Six: Dependent Stance: Head Triad
Seven: Aggressive Stance: Head Triad

Some say you know you've reached your number because you might feel a bit embarrassed by it, you feel "found out." Richard Rohr says, "If you don't sense the whole thing as somehow humiliating, you haven't yet found your number."

There can be plenty of ah-ha moments too when you begin to dive deep into motivations and fears.

The Enneagram is a powerful and fascinating guide into understanding the multifaceted regions of our self and our behavior. Through study, discernment, and life experience, our understanding of it can enrich our self-knowledge for years to come.

THREE

Reflective writing as self-guided meditation and psychotherapy

As discussed in the first section of this book, meditation is a powerful form of working on developing calm, breaking down egoic layers, and helping us access other parts of ourselves. We have developed an activity that we think of as a crossroads between meditation and therapy.

We sometimes offer this framework as a workshop for building self-knowledge. The path toward self-actualization — toward becoming a Big Self — begins with the self. Not navel-gazing. Not selfish entropy. Not analysis paralysis. No, the journey of understanding the world, your place in it, how you interact with others, and their blind spots and strengths, begins with understanding your own blinds spots and strengths.

We advocate an approach to building self-knowledge that engages with what you're feeling and thinking, not letting go. Similar to meditation, it requires a focus of attention. This powerful approach to self-understanding is expressed through writing. Writing is not only for writers. Writing is for all of us. As Julia Cameron notes in her book *The Right to Write: An Invitation and Initiation into the Writing Life*, "I believe we all come into life as writers."

Writing helps us track our spinning thoughts and feelings, which can lead to key insights. Most of us do not think in complete sentences but in self-interrupted, looping, impressionistic fragments. Writing documents thoughts that are otherwise fleeting and transparent. Writing speaks to another consciousness, in this case, another part of the self.

Writing also creates a mind-body-spirit connection; it is a fully immersive experience with the self. When you use your hands to write something directly from your brain, you are creating a powerful connection between your inner experience and your body's movement out in the world. It is a form to find meaning through feeling and intuition within language. We hold worries, fears, and memories in our bodies. Writing is a small movement, but it can be incredibly powerful when you are writing down what is in your mind.

When practiced regularly, active reflective writing can bring a profound sense of well-being and increased confidence. It has a resonance, lingering in the mind long after the work has been done. This is not "formal" writing, and for that primary reason, this is a practice for everyone, not just those who believe they are writers or even good bookkeepers or diarists.

How it works for practicing on your own

1.

Find a quiet place where you can create the right conditions to think and feel. Aim for 25 minutes. Aim for consistency (at least five times a week as you develop the habit).

Don't get hung up on the length of time. If it is getting in the way of your being consistent, then do what works for you.

For each time-boxed period of writing you are seeking to uncover feelings. You seek to write what you hear, to get down on paper thoughts as if you were speaking to your "self." With a little practice you begin to learn how to direct your thinking. These aren't just freewrites (like Julia Cameron's popular approach in *The Artist's Way*). These aren't "morning pages" where you do a "mind dump" to "drain the oil pan" in order to declutter the mind and get it to a clearer creative source. These also aren't intended to be laborious diaries or journals in which you feel burdened to report the trivialities of the day possibly for some hidden nugget of insight you'd neglected. Those get dull fast.

This is active reflective writing. You're coming to the page with a purpose, and the purpose is to listen. Think of it as meditation, but with an advantage. Like meditation you will need to put into it what you want to get out of it. You will need to develop a regular, disciplined practice in a quiet environment as free from outer distraction as possible. Also, feel free to create the conditions for your environment as suits you and your "self's" ability to focus. If that means lighting a candle, incense, or playing a particular kind of rhythmic instrumental music, by all means, create the rituals that work for you.

2.

Find the kind of music that works for you.

Some like Baroque music because its rhythms are consistently in the range of the human heartbeat. Some prefer certain types of Hindi ragas. Others have their own meditation channels and artists. Find the kind that creates calm, that helps transport you, and slow you down. Find music without words.

3.

Begin with where you are, how you are feeling right now, but adapt as you progress.

Like meditation, active reflective writing can begin with a concept or a theme or an image. When you get into the habit and practice of active reflective writing, you should consider such approaches. At first, however, you should let your mind be free.

When you make a statement, especially regarding an emotion, you might consider asking yourself a question: What do I mean by _____? This inquiry into your emotions releases your mind's anxious thoughts. It slows you down. It helps you dig.

Final suggestions and what to expect

Remember, you are engaging your feelings, giving them attention (they may or may not deserve). Similar to psychotherapeutic approaches, the writing can also lead to personal revelations through the examination of our inner experience, and through them we can put them in perspective and/or heal them.

If you really have no idea how to begin or are generally concerned that these will end up feeling very much like a personal journal and nothing more, consider some well-angled questions to begin with. Think of them as personal inquiries. Ask yourself, "What am I anxious about at this very moment?" Similarly, you could ask yourself what you are upset about, or even excited about?

Think of yourself as a researcher seeking to uncover the sources of your anxieties. Much like we feel when a therapist (often a relative stranger who simply guides us with well-timed questions), we are listening to ourselves and through doing so draining them of their intensity (even if we don't arrive at a deep insight).

While there is tremendous energy for discovering self-knowledge by seeking the sources of our emotional state, sometimes it can begin with a healthy dose of practical unpacking. Sometimes it is satisfying to simply ask yourself what steps you need to confront a person or situation. What do you need to get others to do? What needs to happen and when? It could be that in the present swimming of the moment you can't even get to core emotions other than through generalized anxiety, and practical unpacking and analysis are perfectly in good order.

Some of the benefits we've seen in our students and workshop practitioners is a deeper sense of calm. Sometimes the experience sparks an inner joy and people report feeling energized. It also develops the muscles of focus, a stronger ability to describe and discuss your inner realities, as well as an increase in self-confidence.

Like all building blocks of self-knowledge, active reflective writing brings about changes in people's lives that they didn't expect. Expect the unexpected. Try the method for six weeks, and prepare for some serious results. Not every day will yield huge insights, just as not every day in real life is a banner day. You will have good days and bad.

Other questions people often ask is about the journal. Some suggest no lines, some prefer lines, some prefer certain colored or spaced lines. We don't think it matters. Find what feels comfortable and inviting for you.

At the end of each session think of concluding by reflecting on how you feel, and ideas you have for the next session.

FOUR

Meeting resistance, what to do and what to leave undone

In the first steps to becoming yourself again, or reclaiming yourself, at first you may find a gentle blossoming, a permissive yielding. It will feel beautiful, like seeing a tree animated by a breeze on a warm spring day. But be warned, there are forces that do not want you to be yourself. For many who are consciously aware of those who keep them under their control, this comes as no surprise. For many others who are less conscious, it will.

That's right, it comes from the tyranny of the larger culture. The culture that professes the illusion of consumption and material values, and how we must play the game to always be more until we grind ourselves into nothing, or finally "get there," and realize that "there" is nowhere. It comes from the tyranny of following cultural norms about who wears their hair a certain way, and who dresses in this way or that, and how we behave.

We're endlessly taught how to behave, even with the best of intentions. It also boils down to those nearest and dearest to us. Very few of our parents, relatives, loved ones, or even teachers can honestly say they have no agenda for us.

All that is to say, you must be true to you. The journey toward self-knowledge is the biggest journey. It never ends so long as you take breath and exist on this planet.

One of the most critical skills you need is the ability to find calm. That's the kind of calm we teach (in separate books and courses). We don't teach simplistic "stress reduction techniques." Anyone can look up the "tips and tricks, secrets, and keys to the universe" with a quick Google search. One thing you can't find much of is grounded, reasoned, and thorough discussion, exploration, and practice of critical self-transformation skills, like staying centered and calm.

As Seneca wrote to Lucilius: "Philosophy is not an occupation of a popular nature, nor is it pursued for the sake of self-advertisement. Its concern is not with words, but with facts. It is not carried on with the object of passing the day in an entertaining sort of way and taking the boredom out of leisure. It molds and builds the personality, orders one's life, regulates one's conduct, shows one what one should do and what one should leave undone, sits at the helm and keeps one on the correct course as one is tossed about in perilous seas. Without it no one can lead a life free of fear or worry. Every hour of the day countless situations arise that call for advice, and for that advice we have to look to philosophy."

What does Seneca mean by philosophy? We take it to mean the core building blocks of the Big Self School. We take it to mean the appropriate action toward life. He means, ultimately, living a principled life, a life guided by virtuous actions, and a conscious one.

Notice how he also advises Lucilius to discern the difference between things one should do and things "one should leave undone."

Some questions are not resolvable. Others take time. Don't rush for answers. Keep an open mind and spirit. Stay curious.

Qui n'avance pas, recule

"Qui n'avance pas, recule" is translated as, "Who does not move forward, recedes (or moves backward)." There can be no standstill in your life's journey and your personal growth. There is either evolution or devolution. To be stagnant is the same as to recede.

"Expect poison from stagnant water," as William Wordsworth once wrote. You were meant to remain in motion. Have a mind like water, and you will always be growing in self-understanding.

And when you build up enough water, you need to release, you need to outward flow as well as inward. Remaining actively engaged in your growth and self-understanding will keep you alive and strong and wise, no matter your age, all the rest of the days of your life.

THE BIG SELF SCHOOL

The Big Self School is a personal growth learning community, whose central mission is to help you deepen your self-knowledge so that you can improve your life. We create digital courses, online community, books, and media designed to activate self-awareness, deeper connections, bold action, and healthy habits so you can play big without burning out.

www.bigselfschool.com

ABOUT THE AUTHOR

Chad Prevost has advanced degrees in creative writing, literature, and theology. A workshop leader and entrepreneur, he has started and participated in writing and literary arts communities in Atlanta, Austin, Chattanooga, and New York. He also has experience writing as a journalist for startups in tech and logistics. He is the author of several books of poetry, as well as interactive-fiction for young adults. He has innovated writing processes to foster reflection and insight, narrative strength, and authentic voice since 2004. Chad supports the Oxford Comma.